# Ponds
## and pond life

ANITA GANERI

Illustrated by Jamie Medlin

FRANKLIN WATTS
NEW YORK • LONDON • TORONTO • SYDNEY

© 1993 Franklin Watts

Published in the United States
in 1993 by
Franklin Watts, Inc.
95 Madison Avenue
New York, NY 10016

Library of Congress Cataloging-in-Publication Data

Ganeri, Anita, 1961–
    Ponds and pond life / by  Anita Ganeri
        p.  cm. — (Nature detective)
    Includes index.
    Summary: Introduces pond life through the seasons by looking at
the insects, mammals, birds, and flowers that live in and around ponds.
    ISBN 0-531-14226-4
    1. Pond fauna—Juvenile literature. 2. Pond ecology—Juvenile
literature. [1. Pond animals. 2. Pond ecology. 3. Ecology.] I. Title.
II. Series: Nature detective (New York, N.Y.)
QL146.3.G36 1993                                        92-6263
574.909'692—dc20                                        CIP AC

Designer: Splash Studio
Editor: Sarah Ridley
Additional illustrations: Terry Pastor

Consultants: Many thanks to
Nigel Hester and Michael Chinery for
all their help with the book.

Printed in Belgium

# Contents

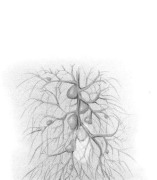

# What is a pond?

A pond is a small area of fresh, still water. It may lie in a natural hollow, carved out by an ancient glacier or worn away by wind and rain, or in a man-made hole. Ponds vary in shape and size. Some are little more than large puddles that have filled with rain. Others are more like small lakes. But they are all shallow enough for plants to grow in, with their roots anchored in the muddy pond bottom.

Ponds are fascinating places to watch nature. They are among the richest habitats on earth, providing homes for a huge variety of plants and animals. Is there a pond near you? You may even have a pond in your backyard. Ponds were once much more common than they are today. Many have been used as trash heaps or drained to create dry land. But those that remain are well worth a visit. You will quickly be able to recognize and identify many different pond plants and animals.

## Types of ponds

**Farm ponds**  Many ponds are man-made. Farm ponds were dug or made by damming streams. They were used for geese and ducks, and provided drinking water for the farm animals.

**Village ponds**  In Colonial days, most villages used to have ponds. They provided water for cattle and horses, and became a familiar part of the village scene.

**Park ponds**  Even in the middle of the busiest cities and towns, park ponds give shelter as well as food for ducks, geese, and swans. Watch out in late spring for strings of ducklings following their mothers.

**Backyard ponds**  If you have a pond in your backyard, it will be an ideal place to begin your detective work. Backyard ponds attract insects, frogs, and hungry birds, such as herons.

**Natural ponds**  These can be found in open countryside on mountains, hilltops, and valleys. Gradually they become covered with a thick layer of plants and dead leaves which eventually turn the pond into dry land. All ponds would dry up eventually if they weren't cleaned out.

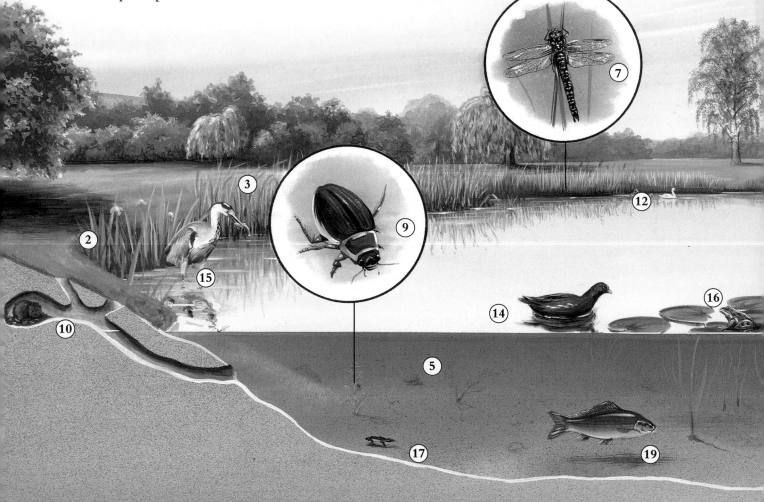

## Ponds and pond life

A sunny, sheltered, pollution-free pond can support a thriving community of plants and animals. They range from tiny, one-celled creatures to fierce, meat-eating fish, such as pickerels. Some are truly aquatic; they spend their whole lives in the water and are specially adapted to help them survive. Others, such as many water birds, may visit the pond to drink, feed, or nest. Look out for tracks around the muddy edges of the pond. They may have been made by visiting foxes or mink.

The plants and animals below are a basic guide to the wide variety of pond life. There is much more information about these different groups throughout this book.

**Pond plants**  Plants such as **1** water lilies, **2** irises, **3** reed grass, **4** cattails, **5** stonewort, and **6** algae.

**Insects**  Including **7** dragonflies, **8** water striders, **9** water scavengers, and others.

**Mammals**  Mammals such as **10** water voles, and others.

**Water birds**  Including **11** mallards, **12** swans, **13** coots, **14** moorhens, and **15** herons.

**Amphibians**  Amphibians such as **16** frogs, toads, and **17** newts. — ins out water

**Fish**  Including **18** sticklebacks, **19** carp, and **20** perch.

**"Minibeasts"**  Minibeasts such as **21** water spiders, **22** pond snails, and **23** swan mussels.

# The pond habitat

A pond is a good example of an ecosystem. This living system is made up of the pond itself (the habitat), and its community of wildlife. The relationships between the various parts of the system are finely balanced. If one part of it is damaged, the rest will be changed and eventually may not survive.

Different plants and animals are found in different areas of the habitat. Every part of the pond and its surroundings are used. Watch for dragonflies and mosquitoes hovering above the water and for whirligig beetles and water striders skimming the surface. Just under the surface, you may be able to see mosquito larvae hanging head down. Birds build their nests among waterside plants and pond snails crawl up the stems of submerged weeds. Frogs and newts may be hiding among the plants. You may catch sight of the shadow of a fish swimming in the open water.

There are also many much smaller areas to live in. These are called microhabitats. Some of them are shown below.

**Plant stems**
Underwater stems are home to pond snails, which graze on their slimy covering of algae. Dragonfly nymphs crawl up the stems of pond plants as they change from pond-living nymphs into flying, land-living adults.

**Stones and pebbles**
Leeches, flatworms, and mayfly nymphs can be found under stones on the pond bottom.

**Mud, silt, and sand** Worms, freshwater clams, fingernail clams, and some insect young burrow into the mud on the pond bottom. Some caddisfly larvae use grains of sand to build protective coats around their soft bodies (see page 15).

**Floating leaves** The underside of floating leaves, such as water lily pads, provide perfect egg-laying sites for pond snails and insects. They also provide shelter from the hot sun for fish, and convenient resting places for frogs. Many small algae and hydras also thrive underneath leaves.

## What do pond creatures eat?

In the pond community, all the animals rely on the plants, directly or indirectly, for their food. Green plants use sunlight to make their own food, by a process called photosynthesis. They are eaten by plant-eating animals, or herbivores. In turn, these provide food for meat-eating animals, called carnivores. The plants and animals are linked together in a food chain. There are many different food chains in a healthy pond. This is just one example.

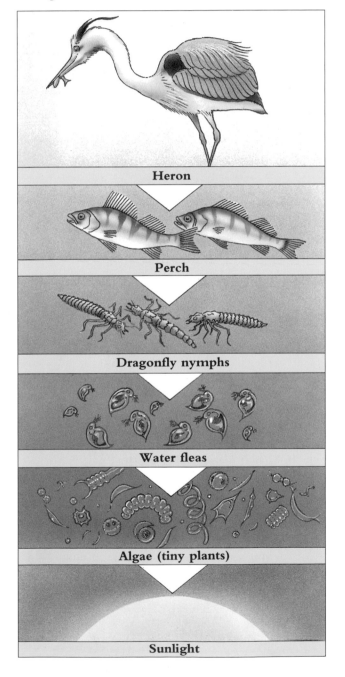

**Heron**

**Perch**

**Dragonfly nymphs**

**Water fleas**

**Algae (tiny plants)**

**Sunlight**

## Pond watching

The best time to go pond watching is in spring or summer when the plants are starting to flower and the animals are having their young. Whenever you go, though, never go on your own. Always take a friend or better still, an adult. Never go in or near the water unless you can swim. If you do want to wade a short way in, test the depth of the water and mud first with a long pole or stick. Avoid swampy patches of ground and slippery rocks or stones. If you go pond watching in winter, never walk across the ice.

The following pieces of equipment will help you to watch and study pond life. If you collect samples, always put them back and replace any logs or stones that you move.

**Field guides** A set of good field guides will help you identify any plants and animals you see.

**Notebook and pencils** Write down the plants and animals you see, with details of their appearance, behavior, and whereabouts in the pond when you saw them. Instead of taking specimens home, do some rough sketches.

**Magnifying glass** A magnifying glass is essential for looking at smaller pond creatures in detail. Choose a lens with a magnification of 10 x.

**Net** You will need a fine-meshed net for collecting and sorting through samples of pond water. You can buy a net, or see page 30 for how to make your own.

**Bucket, jelly jars, plastic tubs, and a shallow dish** These are useful for collecting samples and keeping specimens in. Tie a length of string to the bucket handle so you can pull it through the water. A shallow white plastic dish is ideal for looking at creatures closely, while allowing them to move around.

# Which plants grow in ponds?

Plants are an essential part of the pond community. They not only provide food for the animals, but their stems and leaves also provide shelter and egg-laying sites. The plants that live under the water, the submerged plants, release oxygen as a waste product of photosynthesis. This dissolves in the water, providing vital supplies for pond animals. They are particularly dependent on the plants' oxygen as pond water does not receive fresh oxygen-rich water from streams or rivers.

Pond plants grow in distinct zones around the pond, and on or under the water. They have special features to help them survive in their particular habitat. If you cannot recognize a plant right away, make a note of which zone it is in (marginal, floating, or submerged) and what it looks like. This will make it easier to look up later in your field guide.

## Marginal plants

Plants growing around the pond edge are called marginal plants. Many have strong stems, called rhizomes, that creep horizontally through the mud. This keeps the plants from being blown over by the wind. It also means that the plants can spread very quickly. If they are not controlled, they can turn a pond into marshland.

**Marsh marigold**  This plant has very similar flowers to a buttercup. You can identify the marsh marigold though, by its big, heart-shaped leaves. It likes marshy ground and will grow up to 11 inches tall. It flowers from March to July.

**Reed grass**  Great beds of reeds fringe many ponds. The plants have tough, woody stems and can grow 10 feet high. Reeds often stand with their roots submerged because they need the water to grow. In summer, watch for their feathery brown flowerheads.

## AMAZING FACTS

Over half of the world's oxygen is produced by algae in the sea and in freshwater.

The smallest flowering plant in the world is a type of duckweed, *Wolffia angusta*, of Australia. It is only 1/4 inch long and 1/8 inch wide.

The Amazonian water lily has huge, floating leaves. The largest leaf ever measured was 8 feet wide. The leaves have thick, air-filled ribs on their undersides which help them to float.

**Cattails** These plants are easy to recognize from their velvety brown or tan seed-head spikes. These burst open to release their fluffy white seeds.

## How much oxygen do plants release?

Try this simple experiment to see how much oxygen submerged plants produce during photosynthesis. Put a piece of water weed in a jelly jar of water. Stand it on a sunny windowsill. Watch for the bubbles of oxygen that the plant releases as it starts to photosynthesize. Now shade the jar from the sun for a while. Do the bubbles come off as quickly when the jar is shaded?

**Mare's tail** Mare's tails grow partly submerged in the water with their small leaves growing on the part of the stem that shows above the water. Their stems can grow up to 3 feet tall.

**Water plantain** The pink or white three-petaled flowers of the water plantain appear in July and August. They are closed in the morning and evening, only opening in the afternoon when there are plenty of insects about for pollination.

**Arrowhead** You should be able to spot this plant's arrowhead-shaped leaves quite easily. They poke out of shallow water. The arrowhead also has ribbon-like underwater leaves. Its white and pink flowers show above the water in summer. They have three petals.

**Water mint** This plant is related to the garden mint used in cooking. Crush a leaf between your fingers and see how strong it smells. It has reddish, hairy stems, hairy green leaves, and purple clusters of sweet-smelling flowers.

## Floating plants

Some plants float on the pond surface, with their roots in the bottom mud or trailing in the water. Floating plants are supported by the water, so they do not need strong, rigid stems like land plants. They have large air-filled spaces between their cells to help keep them afloat.

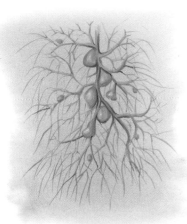

**Greater bladderwort**
Bladderworts are insect-eating plants with no roots that float near to the pond surface. They have little "bladders" on their leaves, with trap-door openings. When an insect brushes against the sensitive bristles around a bladder, the trap-door opens. The insect is sucked inside and digested.

**Water soldier** The water soldier gets its name from its sharp, sword-like leaves. It usually lives underwater, except when it flowers in summer. After flowering, it sinks down deep into the pond to avoid the winter frosts.

**Water crowfoot** Some species of water crowfoot have floating and submerged leaves. The floating ones are flat and broad. The submerged leaves are fine and feathery. The water crowfoot produces its floating flowers in May and June. It is related to the buttercup.

**Broad-leaved pondweed** This is one of the most common species of the pondweed family and has floating leaves, as well as submerged ones. Its long branching rhizome shoots settle in the mud at the bottom of the pond and send up shoots which bear leaves. The floating leaves provide a convenient resting place for many pond creatures, both above and below the surface of the water.

**Water fern** This floating plant has short, thick stems covered in small leaves which overlap like scales. These often turn pinkish-red in autumn.

**Duckweed** These tiny plants spread over the pond surface like a green carpet. Each has a thread-like root dangling down into the water. Duckweed survives winter by sinking to the mud on the pond bottom. As its name suggests, it is eaten by ducks.

## Submerged plants

Submerged plants live mostly underwater. They have fine, feathery leaves for absorbing carbon dioxide from the water. Plants use this gas to make food. They also have fine, flexible stems and leaves which are less likely to be damaged by the water. These underwater plants are the pond's all-important oxygenators, releasing oxygen into the water.

**Water starwort** This plant has long, underwater stems that can grow up to 3 feet long. They also have floating leaves, which form star-shaped groups on the surface of the pond.

**Water weed** This plant has long stems and small green leaves. It grows very fast and can choke ponds if it is not controlled. It is popular with aquarium owners for the amount of oxygen and shelter it provides.

**Water milfoil** Water milfoil is an underwater plant, but its flowers grow above the water. Water milfoil can grow deeper than most other pond plants because it can survive with very little sunlight.

**Stonewort** The stonewort is closely related to algae. It is usually found in chalky water and may be covered in a hard, limy crust. Stoneworts often grow in large clumps. They smell a bit like garlic!

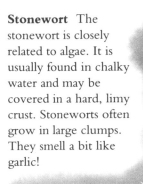

## Pond algae

Algae grow in salt- and freshwater. They are the simplest types of plant and range in size from tiny plants to huge seaweeds. Many pond algae are so small you need a microscope to see them. Others are just visible to the naked eye. In warm sunny weather, the algae may grow very quickly and turn the pond water green. This is a good time to take a sample to study. If the algae grow too much, however, they block out the sunlight. The submerged plants cannot photosynthesize and produce oxygen, and the pond suffocates.

**Spirogyra** This common alga grows in long, green threads that form soft clumps in the pond. The clumps may be free-floating or attached to stones. Spirogyra feels slimy because it has a covering of mucus.

**Diatoms** These are microscopic, single-celled algae. The various species come in a wide range of shapes, from ovals to rods to wheels. They sometimes form a brownish slime on plants and mud at the bottom of the pond.

# Insects of the pond

There are at least a million different species of insects in the world. They are able to live in a very wide range of habitats, including ponds. As a group, insects are quite easy to recognize. They have three parts to their bodies and six legs. Most have wings.

Insects have adapted to live in every part of the pond habitat. Dragonflies hover above the water on the lookout for prey. The surface of the water is the hunting ground of water striders and other bugs and beetles. It also traps insects that others snap up for food. Many insects have larvae that live totally underwater, among the mud and submerged plants. All these insects are pond specialists. They have special ways of moving, feeding, and breathing in their watery environment.

You can watch pond insects throughout the day. In the early morning, insects are sluggish, slow and easy to spot. They have not yet had time to warm up and become active. Look for them on the stems and leaves of pond-side plants. In the early evening, swarms of mosquitoes and gnats emerge, attracting birds such as swallows. The best time of the year for insect-watching is summer, when the insects are busy attracting mates and breeding.

## Breathing

All animals need to breathe oxygen. Some come to the surface of the water to breathe. Others breathe oxygen dissolved in the water. Many underwater larvae breathe through gills, like fish. Other insects have ingenious ways of getting and storing air.

**Rat-tailed maggot**
This maggot is the larva of the drone fly. It lives in fairly shallow water and breathes through its tail. This breathing tube can be extended to a length of 6 inches to reach the surface.

**Water scorpion**   The adult water scorpion lives underwater, among submerged pond plants. Like the rat-tailed maggot, it has a long "snorkel" at the end of its body. This breaks the water surface and takes in air. The snorkel is actually two tubes hooked together.

**Water scavenger**
Many diving beetles live underwater, but visit the surface for air. They trap air among their body hairs and store it under their wings. The water scavenger gets its silvery appearance from the trapped air.

## Feeding

Pond insects feed on plants, tadpoles, and each other. However many adult insects hardly eat anything. But their larvae have huge appetites. If adults do eat, they are sometimes herbivores (plant-eaters), while their nymphs and larvae are carnivores (meat-eaters).

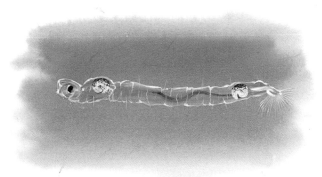

**Dragonfly** Adult dragonflies are skillful hunters. They can catch insect prey in mid-air. "Hawker" dragonflies fly over the water in search of food. "Darters" wait on a perch, then dart out at prey. Dragonfly nymphs live underwater and are fierce carnivores, preying on water fleas, tadpoles, and each other.

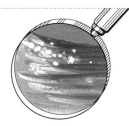

## Testing surface tension

The film covering the surface of water is caused by the water molecules bonding together. This is called surface tension. The film is very fine, but surprisingly strong. To test this, fill a small bowl with water. Float a piece of blotting paper on top of the water, with a paper clip on top of the paper. As the paper gets soggy and sinks, the paper clip will stay in place on the surface. It is supported by the surface film.

The surface film over a pond supports many insects and provides them with a fertile hunting ground.

**Phantom gnat larvae** Adult phantom gnats do not seem to feed at all. Their larvae, however, are carnivores. They snatch and eat anything that swims too close. Phantom gnat larvae are transparent. If you are looking for them in your pond water, it helps to hold your jelly jar against a dark background and shine a light at it from behind.

**Water measurer** This pond insect has very long thin legs for walking on the surface of the pond, in search of food. It feeds on drowned insects floating on the water, as well as water fleas and other small pond insects, which it stabs through the surface of the water

## AMAZING FACTS

The larvae of *Nymphula*, or china mark, moths live underwater inside tents which they make from pieces of floating plants, such as water lily leaves.

The world's largest dragonfly, *Megaloprepus caeruleata*, has a body over 7½ inches long and a wingspan of up to 5 inches.

Some female giant water bugs lay their eggs on the males' backs. They are stuck in place with a waterproof, glue-like substance. The female then flies off, leaving the male behind to care for the eggs until they hatch.

## Movement

Insects move to find food and to escape from danger. Many pond insects have special features to help them move on or through the water. These features are a useful guide to identification.

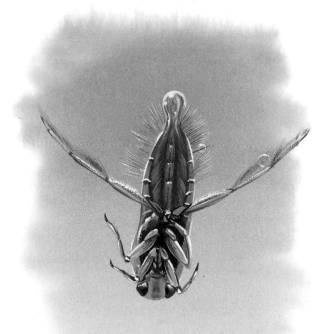

**Whirligig beetle**
Groups of whirligig beetles spin around and around on the surface of the pond using their very short paddlelike legs. They are searching for insects to eat. Each of their eyes is divided in two. One part is used for looking over the surface of the water, while the other looks down into the water.

**Springtail**  Springtails cannot fly but have another way of escaping enemies. They have forked tails which are usually folded under their bodies. These tails can be flicked down to enable them to leap high into the air and escape from predators. They can jump up to 1 foot high.

**Backswimmer**  As its name suggests, the backswimmer swims on its back, using its long back legs as oars. Both these features make this an easy insect to recognize. It lives under the water but regularly surfaces to renew its air supply. It is a fierce carnivore, preying on tadpoles, insects, and even small fish.

**Water strider**  These bugs are adapted for moving at high speed over the delicate film that covers the surface of the water. They row themselves along, using their four back legs. Their feet are covered in pads of waxy hairs which repel water and keep the insects from sinking. Water striders feed on smaller insects that get trapped in the surface film. They grasp their prey with their shorter front legs.

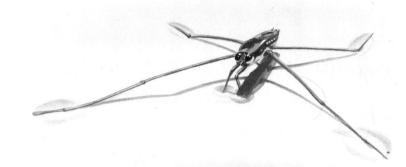

# The life history of a pond insect

Insects start life as eggs, but they go through a series of amazing changes before they finally emerge as adults. This process of change is called metamorphosis. Many pond insects change from eggs into larvae, then into pupae, and finally into adults. Some, such as dragonflies, do not have a pupal stage. Their young are called nymphs.

Many pond insects have aquatic larvae, although they spend their adult lives out of the water.

## Caddisfly metamorphosis

1. The female caddisfly crawls underwater to lay her eggs. They are protected inside a jelly-like bag, attached to a stone or plant stem.

2. The larvae hatch after about two weeks. They then make themselves protective cases out of grains of sand, bits of plant, shells, or stones. They crawl along the bottom of the pond, feeding on plants.

3. After about a year, the larvae seal both ends of their cases and turn into pupae. Inside the cases, their bodies break down and are reconstructed in adult form. A caddisfly spends about two weeks as a pupa.

4. When the adult is ready to emerge, the pupa bites its way out of its case. Then the pupa climbs up a plant stem and out of the water.

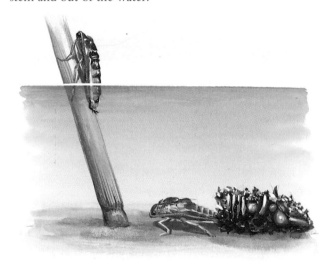

5. Its skin splits and the adult struggles out and flies away. Adult caddisflies only live for about a month.

# Pond mammals

Very few mammals are true pond dwellers. But some, such as water shrews, spend a lot of time in the water and have webbed feet and waterproof fur to help them. Other mammals, such as weasels and rats, are attracted to the water to feed on the fish, plants, or swarms of insects. The rushes and reeds around the pond shelter land mammals, such as mice and shrews, which themselves attract other predatory mammals.

You need to be patient to watch pond mammals. Most of them are very shy and keep well out of sight. Some are nocturnal – they only come out at night to hunt for food or drink from the pond. If you do go mammal watching, keep very quiet and stay out of the wind. Pond mammals have excellent senses of hearing and smell and will easily detect you and run away long before you detect them.

**Bat** In summer, large swarms of insects attract certain bats to the pond. They fly fast and low over the water, catching insects in mid-air or picking them off the surface.

**Water shrew** Water shrews are good swimmers, diving after their prey of insects, fish, and frogs. Despite their small size, they have huge appetites and are fierce hunters. They can paralyze larger prey with their poisonous saliva. They also walk along the bottom of the pond, looking for food. Some species have stiff hairs around their feet, toes, and tail. These trap air and help the shrews to swim.

**Mink** Mink are related to weasels, and have the same long bodies, short legs, and small ears. They have partially webbed feet and are good swimmers. They come out at night to feed on frogs, birds, fish, and other pond mammals. Many wild mink are descendents of those that escaped from fur farms.

**Nutria** Nutrias originally come from South America but were introduced into other countries for their valuable fur. Some escaped and formed wild communities. They are strong swimmers, well adapted for life in the water. They can close their nostrils when they dive to keep water from getting in. They are vegetarian, feeding mainly on reeds and other plants.

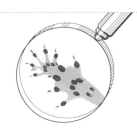

## Tracking mammals

Although you might not see the mammals themselves, you can keep a lookout for any clues they leave behind. These may include droppings, leftover bits of food, burrows or nests, and tracks. The best place to find tracks is in the damp, pond-side mud or in the snow. Measure and draw the tracks, making a note of the pattern they make. Can you tell which animals made the tracks? Use a field guide to help you.

## Water vole

The first sign you may have of a water vole is a loud "plop" as it dives head first into the water. Water voles are strong swimmers, paddling along with a sort of dog-paddle stroke. They dive to escape from predators, such as herons. They also stir up the mud on the pond bottom to give themselves a protective screen.

Water voles are mainly vegetarian, but they also eat snails and worms. They leave behind patches of nibbled grass or reeds on the pond bank.

A hole in the bank may lead to a water vole's complex burrow system. It has an underwater entrance too. Voles often graze the grass around the bankside entrance, leaving a neat, circular "lawn." The burrow leads to a chamber with a nest of chewed-up grass where the vole raises its young. There are other chambers for storing acorns and beechnuts for winter.

Water voles can be mistaken for rats which also visit ponds and are good swimmers. But water voles have more rounded faces, and shorter tails and ears than rats.

# Water birds

Ponds attract a wide variety of birds, for many different reasons. Some birds live permanently near ponds. Others use ponds as egg-laying sites or visit to feed, drink, and bathe. Temporary visitors include some species of geese who fly down from the far north and spend the winter near ponds further south.

## Dabblers and divers

Ducks are the most common pond birds and should be easy to spot. One way of telling them apart is by their methods of feeding. Some ducks dive for food. Others skim the surface of the water with their beaks. They are called dabbling ducks.

## Dabbling ducks

**Pintail** Pintails get their name from the males' long tail feathers. Females do not have these plumes. Pintails have long necks and beaks to help them dabble for water plants and small pond creatures.

Many water birds have lost their wild homes as country ponds have been drained to create more land. Some have adapted to life in cities and towns. You will probably see ducks, geese, and even swans on a visit to your local park. This is a good place to study the birds more closely. Remember never to disturb the birds, especially if you visit in spring or summer when they are breeding.

**Mallard** Mallard ducks feed mainly on water plants and seeds. They skim their wide, flat beaks across the pond surface, sieve out any food and pump the water out again. They also up-end in the pond to find food in deeper water. Many mallards in county parks are tame enough to feed from your hand.

**Teal** The teal also dabbles for plants, seeds, and small pond creatures. It is a graceful swimmer, but only rarely dives. Teals are sociable birds, often forming large flocks.

## Diving duck

**Tufted duck** Diving ducks have a distinctive method of takeoff, by running along the surface of the water. Tufted ducks do a little jump before they dive down to between 3-4 feet, searching for underwater food. They stay under for about 15 seconds at a time. They eat water plants, insects, and shellfish. The male has a larger "tuft" than the female and also has a white rectangle of feathers on each side of its body.

## Another diving bird

**Red-necked grebe**
Grebes are also diving birds. The red-necked grebe has a long neck which it uses to catch fish underwater. It can dive very quickly and quietly, and can stay under water for up to 40 seconds.

## Feet for swimming and walking

Birds that spend most or all of their lives near water have specially adapted feet for swimming and walking on soft surfaces. Look out for their tracks in the soft mud around the pond edge or in soft winter snow.

**Mute swan** Swans, ducks, and geese have webbed feet that act as paddles to make swimming easier. Swans are strong swimmers but they walk clumsily on land. They patter their feet on the water to help them take off and also use them to brake as they come in to land.

**Moorhen** Moorhens have long thin toes to keep them from sinking into the soft mud around the pond. The long toes also help them to walk over lily pads.

**Coot and grebe** Coots and grebes have scaly lobes of skin between their toes. These help the birds to swim but also prevent them from sinking into the soft mud around the pond.

19

# Food and drink

The swarms of insects around many ponds attract great numbers of birds. Other birds are specialist fish-eaters or come to the pond to drink.

**Mute swan** Swans feed by stretching their neck under the water to fish for food. They also up-end in the water to search for food. Swans feed on insects, crustaceans, mollusks and plants. When they have a clump of plants in their beak, they will lift their head up and sieve the water out through the edges of their beak.

**Heron** Herons hunt from the edge of the pond. They wait patiently for fish to swim past, then grab them with their long, pointed beaks. They catch frogs and tadpoles in the same way. Herons usually fish in the early morning or evening. They often steal goldfish from backyard ponds.

**Swallow** Swallows and swifts are frequent visitors to ponds. They arrive at dawn or dusk when there are plenty of insects to eat. They are skillful fliers, swooping low over the water to pick insects off the surface. They also drink on the wing, dipping their lower beak into the water as they fly across it.

## Eggs and nests

For many water birds, pond-side plants provide sheltered spots in which to lay their eggs and raise their young. They provide nest-building materials too. Other birds make use of different parts of the pond.

**Mallard** Mallards lay their eggs from March to May, in shallow nests of stems and leaves on the ground. The eggs are concealed and kept warm by soft down from the mother's breast. Female mallards are much drabber than the male, or drake. This is to camouflage them as they sit on their nests.

**Coot** Coots use water plants, such as reeds, to build their floating, saucer-shaped nests. These are usually hidden among the reed beds at the water's edge. The nests are raised up to keep the eggs out of the water. The female lays 5-10 buff and brown eggs. They hatch after about three weeks and the chicks leave the nest a few days later.

**Kingfisher** Kingfishers usually live near rivers, but are sometimes seen diving for fish in ponds and lakes. They build their nest deep in the bank at the end of a long tunnel. Their eggs are bright white since they do not need to be camouflaged.

## Water bird watching

When you are watching water birds, wear dull colors and move quietly. Binoculars are very useful for any kind of bird-watching. Many birds are most active in the early morning.

You can also look for clues that birds have left behind. Look for white or greenish-gray droppings at the pond edge. Summer is a good time to do this, when the water recedes over the mud. Keep an ear out for bird sounds, such as the familiar quacking of ducks or the short kik-kik-kik of coots. With practice, you may be able to recognize some water birds from their sounds alone.

## AMAZING FACTS

Tundra swans have over 25,000 feathers - more than any other birds. Over 20,000 of these feathers are on the head and neck.

The Indian cotton teal, or Indian pygmy goose, is the smallest duck in the world. Adults can be as little as 12 inches long, about half the length of a mallard.

Jacanas have toes up to 3 inches long to help them walk over water lily leaves without sinking. This has earned them the nickname "lily trotters."

# Frogs, toads, and newts

Frogs, toads, and newts are amphibians – animals that lead a double life. They are born in the pond, but spend most of their adult lives on land. Adult amphibians never stray very far from the water, however. Some breathe through their skin, as well as with their lungs. They have to keep their skin moist in order for them to absorb oxygen properly.

Frogs, toads, and newts hibernate during the winter. The spring is the best time to look for them, when they are breeding. They are more active at night than during the day. Listen for the mating calls of male frogs and toads. Look for young frogs and toads leaving the pond for the first time. If you do visit a pond at night, always go with an adult. Move slowly and quietly so that you do not disturb the animals.

## Frog or toad?

Frogs and toads look very similar, but there are several ways of telling them apart. Frogs tend to have smoother skins than toads. A toad's skin may be covered in lumpy warts. Frogs have longer legs than toads, for jumping. Toads are able to live in drier places than frogs, further away from the pond.

Newts are easy to recognize, with their streamlined bodies and long tails. They need to stay close to water all the time.

## Avoiding predators

Pond amphibians eat insects, small pond creatures, and each other's tadpoles and spawn. But they are under constant threat from predators, such as pickerels and herons. Some have special means of self-defense.

**Toad**  Under attack, a toad will puff itself up to look bigger and scarier than it actually is. If this does not work, it secretes a foamy, white poison from its skin. The predator will quickly drop its foul-tasting catch. If you touch a toad, always wash your hands afterward.

Toad

Frog

**Great crested newt**  Glands in this newt's moist skin produce a strong-smelling chemical which irritates the skin of most predators. It does not seem to work on grass snakes, however. Smooth newts do not have this defense but they feed at night to avoid predators. Newts can grow new limbs if any are bitten off by an enemy.

**Great crested newt**

**Common newt**

## A frog's life

1. In February or March, adult frogs return to the pond to breed. The male clings tightly to the female while they are mating,

2. The female of some species lays over 2,000 eggs, or spawn. The male fertilizes the eggs as they are being laid. The eggs are coated in jelly for protection and float near the surface of the pond.

3. About 10 days later, tiny fish-like tadpoles hatch out of the eggs. Like fish, they breathe through gills, taking in oxygen dissolved in the water.

4. Over the next 10-12 weeks, the tadpoles gradually develop limbs and lungs and their tails start to shrink. At the end of this time, they turn into tiny frogs. These are now ready to leave the pond for the first time and begin their adult life on land.

5. The tiny frog is called a froglet. Frogs shed their skins, or molt, several times as they grow into adults. In about three years, they are fully grown.

## Toad tadpoles

Toads often return to the ponds of their birth to breed. They lay their eggs in strings up to 10 feet long. The strings are often wound around underwater plant stems. Toads spawn about a month after frogs. Many of their eggs are eaten by frog tadpoles.

## Courting newts

During the breeding season, male newts become more brightly colored. The great crested newt's belly turns orange and red, and black patches swell on the inner surfaces of thighs and feet. It also develops a pattern of spots on its crest. Male newts perform underwater courtship dances to win females. The female lays her eggs singly on pond plants. They take about two weeks to hatch.

## Hatching frog spawn

To see how tadpoles hatch out of eggs, collect a small amount of frog spawn from a pond. Take it home in a jar of pond water, and transfer it into an aquarium (see page 31). Keep the aquarium in a light place (but out of direct sunlight) and make sure it is well stocked with fresh water and pond plants. When the tadpoles hatch, take them straight back to the pond so that they can develop into frogs.

# Which fish live in ponds?

Many types of fish live in freshwater, but only a few can survive in ponds. This is because fish, like all other animals, need to breathe oxygen, and pond water is not as rich in oxygen as river or lake water. Some ponds may also dry up in summer, making life impossible for most fish.

The fish that do live in ponds feed on the pond plants and animals and tend to be slow-moving species. Some prefer the shallow water around the edge of the pond. Others live deep down in the open water. Look for their dark shapes in the water as they move around. In summer, you may see groups of fish gathering in the shallows to lay their eggs.

## Breathing underwater

Fish use gills to breathe oxygen dissolved in the pond water. There is a set of gills on either side of the fish's body, covered by a flap of skin. A fish swims along opening and closing its mouth. As it opens its mouth, it closes its gill covers and gulps in water. Then it closes its mouth, opens its gill covers and pushes the water out again. As the water passes over the gills, blood vessels absorb oxygen and release waste carbon dioxide into the water to be pumped out.

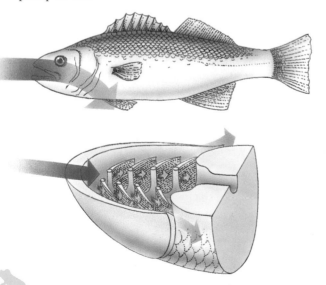

## Three-spined stickleback

The three-spined stickleback is one of very few fish which lay their eggs in a nest. The male builds the nest out of weeds and algae in late spring. Then he dances in front of it to attract her to the nest where she lays her eggs. Several different females lay their eggs in a male's nest. He fertilizes them, then guards them for several weeks until they hatch.

During breeding time, the male's belly and throat turn bright orange-red. He chases away similarly colored rivals.

## Fish watching

Fish watching can be difficult as fish are very timid, but it is well worth the effort. If it is a sunny day, find a shady spot on the bank, or wear a pair of polarized sunglasses to cut down the glare from the water. Crawl on all fours toward the water's edge - this prevents your shadow from falling over the water and scaring the fish off. Move very carefully - fish are highly sensitive to vibrations. Look for any shapes or movements in the water. You can try to tempt the fish to the surface with a few pieces of bread.

**Common carp** Carp mainly feed on the bottom of the pond, where they sift through the mud for insect larvae and worms. They have two sets of barbels at the corners of their mouth to help them feel for food. On hot days, carp like to come to the surface and bask in the sun. Carp can survive in ponds with low levels of oxygen.

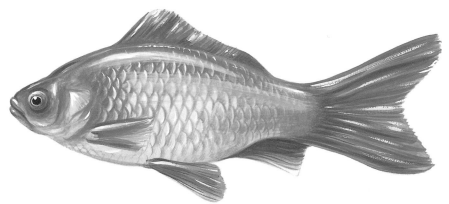

**Goldfish** Goldfish are members of the carp family, and are common in backyard ponds. Most goldfish today are golden orange but their wild ancestors were dull greenish-brown. Goldfish originally came from China and Japan.

**Perch** These fish like clean pond water, shaded by bankside vegetation. Their dark stripes camouflage them among the water weeds. They feed on insects, small fish, worms, and mollusks. Perch spawn in late April and May.

**Pickerel** Pickerel usually prefer quiet rivers or shallow lakes, but can be found in large ponds. Here you may spot them lurking in the pond shallows, looking like small, floating logs. They are fierce carnivores, with mouthsful of sharp teeth for catching their prey of fish, frogs, newts, and even ducklings. They hunt by sight, so prefer clear water with good visibility. When prey is seen, they dart out and grab it. Pickerel can grow up to 4 feet long.

# Minibeasts in the pond

A huge number of small creatures live in ponds, ranging from tiny, one-celled animals to spiders and snails. Pond "minibeasts" live buried in the mud, under stones, on plant stems, and even between grains of sand. They are fascinating to study, but you will need a magnifying glass to see some of them in detail. They play an important role in the pond community, providing food for many larger creatures. Some also help to break down decaying matter that sinks to the bottom of the pond.

## Tiny creatures

**Paramecium**  These one-celled animals live on the bacteria which break down decaying plants in the pond. Rows of hairlike cilia over their bodies help them to swim. They seem to spread from one pond to another in the drops of water sticking to birds and other animals. To see if a sample of pond water contains paramecium, hold your jelly jar against a dark background. The paramecium will show up as darting, see-through specks.

**Green hydra**  Hydra are animals that look like plants. They hang from stones or plants, waving their tentacles to catch particles of food in the water. The tentacles have stinging cells on them which paralyze their prey. If disturbed, they contract into little green blobs. Leave some water weed in a jar of pond water for a while to see if there are any hydra attached. They will unfurl when they feel safe. Green hydra get their color from the tiny algae living inside them.

## Crustaceans and mollusks

**Water flea**  In spring, these tiny crustaceans drift in large swarms near the surface of the water. They move with sudden, jerky jumps. They feed on minute bacteria and algae. In turn, they provide the staple food of many pond carnivores, including insect-eating bladderwort plants (see page 10).

**Seed shrimp**  Weedy ponds are good places to find these crustaceans. They have bean-shaped shells and range in color from white to green or brown. They grow about ¾ inch long. Look for them under stones and in the bottom mud.

**Cyclops**  These creatures are often seen with water fleas. They are about ⅛ inch long, with a single black or red eye in the middle of their head. This has earned them their name, the same name as the one-eyed monsters of ancient Greek legend.

**Great ramshorn snail** This snail is named after the shape of its shell, which resembles a curly ram's horn. It is usually found in larger ponds. It lays its eggs in a flat mass attached to an underwater plant. The snail is usually brown in color, but albino see-through snails can sometimes be found.

**Giant pond snail** Pond snails crawl over the stems and leaves of underwater plants, grazing on the layer of algae on them. The giant pond snail also eats small fish. It breathes air, like a land snail, and sometimes crawls upside down under the surface film, taking oxygen into its lung. The snails lay their eggs in jellylike strings underneath floating leaves.

**Swan mussel** This mollusk usually lies half buried in the mud on the bottom of the pond. It can grow over 8 inches long. It feeds by filtering food from the water. You may sometimes find empty mussel shells on the pond shore.

## Pond dipping

take a sample of the mud on the bottom of the pond. Leave it to settle for a while, then see how many little animals crawl out of it.

The best way of investigating pond life is to go pond dipping. See page 9 for the best equipment to take with you.

Sweep your net through the water and empty your catch into a jelly jar or tub filled with pond water. Let the mud settle, then examine and make notes about any creatures you have caught. Use your magnifying glass to look for details. Put the animals back after you have looked at them. Then

# Worms and leeches

**Fish leech** Leeches are related to earthworms and are a reddish-green color. Some suck blood; others feed on small pond animals. You can easily recognize them by their suckers, one at each end of their bodies. They use these suckers to cling to their prey, or to rocks or plants.

Fish leeches can grow up to 2 inches long. They attach themselves to fish and stay there for a few days, sucking their blood. Small fish may have three or four leeches on their bodies, but a large carp may be covered in up to a hundred leeches at a time.

**Tubifex worm** These thin, red worms live head-down in tubes of mud on the bottom of the pond. You may be able to see these from the surface. They filter food from the mud. They wave their tails to get more oxygen from the water. Each worm is about 1 inch long.

**Hair worm** Hair worms are found in tangled clumps of up to a hundred worms. Each worm can grow up to 2 feet long, but only 1/8 inch wide. Legend says that they were hairs from a horse's tail which had fallen into the water and come alive.

**Flatworm** These worms have soft, flat bodies. They swim along the bottom of the pond by beating their body hairs in the water. They may be white, brown, gray or almost transparent. They feed on living or dead pond animals.

# Spiders and mites

**Fisher spider** Fisher spiders lie in wait on floating leaves, dangling one leg in the water. If they detect vibrations in the water made by insect prey, they race across the water, grab the insect, and take it back to the leaf to eat. The spiders are attached by a silk thread to the leaf so that they can get back safely.

**Water mite** Water mites are related to spiders. Adults are always on the move, rushing about over decaying plants in the pond. They are carnivores, feeding on a range of small animals. Some species are bright red, making them easy to spot. Their eggs are red, too. They are laid on stones or plants.

**Water spider** The water spider of Europe is the only spider that lives underwater. It has an ingenious way of getting enough air to breathe. The spider spins a domed web between underwater plant stems. Then it fills it with air from the surface, trapped in bubbles on its body. This diving bell is the spider's life-support system. It feeds, mates, and lays its eggs inside the bell, leaving only to hunt for fish and insects.

## AMAZING FACTS

Medicinal leeches are so-called because they were once used by doctors to draw blood from patients. This blood-letting was believed to help relieve fevers and other illnesses.

A medicinal leech can suck up to five times its own weight in blood in one go. This will last it for up to one year.

Pond snails' shells usually spiral to the right.

If a pond starts to dry up, many of the one-celled creatures (the protozoa) build up tough "cases" around their bodies for protection. They may be blown far from the pond by the wind and reappear, as if by magic, in damp bogs or fields.

# More things to do

## Surveying a pond

Surveying a pond through the changing seasons is one of the best ways of studying its wildlife. Measure across and around the pond with lengths of string. Then draw a map of its shape. Mark the different plant zones on the map (see pages 8–11) and add any animals you see. You could show the plants and animals with symbols and then repeat and explain them in a key.

Repeat your survey every three months and see how much your map changes.

## Saving a pond

Many ponds are being destroyed by pollution or are being drained to create new land. Whenever this happens, plants and animals lose their natural homes. See if there is a pond near you which needs saving. Then get a group of friends and relatives to help you clear it of garbage and make it a safe habitat again. Wear gloves to pick up any trash and be careful not to hurt yourself on broken glass or crushed cans. Always test the depth of the water and mud first before you step in to the pond. Keep to the edge of the pond, for safety's sake.

## Grow your own marsh

A marsh is formed when some of the plants in and around a pond grow and clog up the water, and gradually turn the pond into land. To make your own marsh, you will need a plastic pond

## Making a net

A strong net is essential for pond dipping (see page 27). You can buy a net from a fishing tackle shop or use a fine-meshed kitchen sieve. But you can make your own net just as easily. You will need a wire coat hanger, a long length of garden stake or a broom handle, and some fine netting from a hardware store.

Bend the coat hanger into a circle and wind the ends around the stake or tie them on with string. Sew the net around the wire circle with string or strong thread. Then tie off the bottom of the net with a double knot.

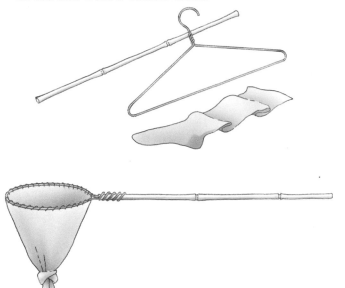

liner. You can buy one from a garden center or a home improvement store. Fill it with peat and soil, then water it well. Plant a selection of irises, rushes, reeds, marsh marigolds, water mint, and water plantain. Water your marsh frequently so that it does not dry out.

1          2          3

## Making an underwater viewer

Instead of taking samples, you may prefer to watch pond creatures in their underwater homes.

1. To make an underwater viewer, you will need a large plastic yogurt cup or plastic flower pot, some clear plastic wrap, and a rubber band.

2. Cut the top and bottom off the pot and cover the sharp edges with tape.

3. Cover one end with the plastic wrap, held in place by the rubber band. Hold the viewer just under the water surface and look through the uncovered end.

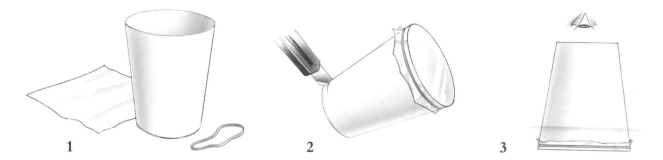

1                              2                              3

## Making a freshwater aquarium

A simple aquarium is the ideal place for studying how pond creatures, especially insects and snails, move and behave. You can buy a clear fish tank or aquarium from a pet store. Put some sand and gravel on the bottom and fill the tank with pond water, or a mixture of pond and tap water. Add some larger stones, and use them to weight down pieces of pond plants and weeds. Put the aquarium in a well-lit place, but not in direct sunlight.

After a few days, add some pond insects or other small creatures. You could also add some pond snails and watch them crawl over the sides of the tank. Keep the tank covered in order to stop your insects from flying away.

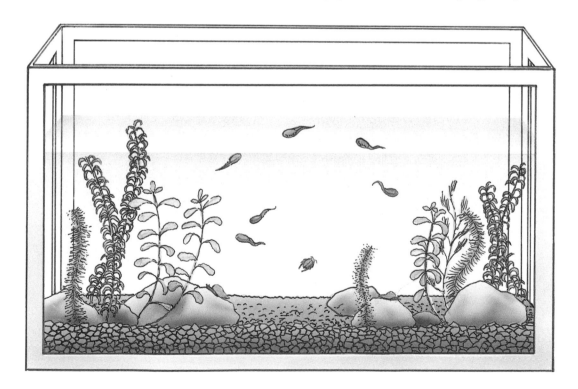

# Index

PRINTED IN BELGIUM BY proost
INTERNATIONAL BOOK PRODUCTION